# THANKS FOR NOTHING

*poems by*

# Deb Jannerson

*Finishing Line Press*
Georgetown, Kentucky

# THANKS FOR NOTHING

## ACKNOWLEDGMENTS

Poems from this collection first appeared in the following:

@ARoomofHerOwn on Twitter: "morning machine"
*Cardinal Sins*: "dolores"
*E·ratio*: "no soliciting"
*Esoterotica's Third Anthology: Longing*, ed. Shadow Angelina Starkey: "dear jessica"
*Inklette*: "orange day"
*The Ocotillo Review*: "sprung"
The Telepoem Booth: "flight"

Though unpublished, "space between" received Honorable Mention for the 2017
Gival Press Oscar Wilde Award.



Publisher: Leah Maines

Editor: Christen Kincaid

Cover Art: Mia O. Savage

Author Photo: Steve Hammond

Cover Design: Elizabeth Maines McCleavy

Printed in the USA on acid-free paper.
Order online: www.finishinglinepress.com
            also available on amazon.com

Author inquiries and mail orders:
Finishing Line Press
P. O. Box 1626
Georgetown, Kentucky 40324
U. S. A.

# Table of Contents

*For Kelsey, always*

**how long have you been suffering from agoraphobia?**

you've misunderstood.

despite the diplomas tiling your mortar in
curves to accommodate the meticulously
researched non-threatening room, you
cannot grasp the onionskins of my present, the
individual scroll of wacky tales
handled only by the narrator, the
alchemical allowance of exceptionalism, the way
each strike in my timeline has compounded into
a subway roar.

a corner click of curiosity buried
beneath my sternum murmurs,
*oh*,
but it is quickly shunned.

the shield of reaction jumps to my
ad hominem defense:
you've misunderstood.
i compile no mountains of once-cheesy boxes,
do not have my two-hundred calorie chicken
spirited to my moonlit doorstep,
am not a protagonistic shell awaiting the
healing of his frightened mind
by love.

i leave the brick box certain i have made my point.

tomorrow, i will drift conscious in mid-afternoon,
hazy as two, hazy as ten, and
remember the certain line of your mouth, the
glass-bottomed bubble of your
seasoned nuance, the
magnified honeycomb of each
comforting cliché once it becomes
intimate and dimensioned,
and i'll cry.

**of all the feelings i did not miss**

in the calendars of caterpillar progress
as the legislators relaxed their thumbs
and the prism grew promise, a proper pixilated projection

in the choruses who foresaw freedom
as our frayed vocal cords unknotted
and set sail into the strained semi-sight of safety

in the moons of murky links ignited
as building rallies sparked from stone
and hungered to hear halting half-ballooned hope

the worst is this spinning, fruitless anger
saturating the air of my country cage.

**sweeps**

the child whose parents hurt her
appeared in only one episode per show,
a ghostly reincarnation clad in a
fluid one-syllable name, who
dissolved from existence when the
main kid confessed to his parents, when he
did the right thing.

a generation of bit-chomping
laughtracked child stars
descended, the rhythm of would-be waves
falling in sweeps, the corner of
one good eye peeled like a
sandwich wrapper, awaiting one's
heroic, humbling
growing pain of the week.

the neutrality of first person
made alien the gamble of
scuffed shell as self,
spared personhood for point, casting
the plucky protagonist as everyman,
relegating the case study to a brief pet bunny with
an offscreen nametagged villain
more fable than father.

on the other side of the screen, she
followed her peers at a
distance, prepared for the smear of
cake-sticky makeup under a dark eye,
for the rug burn-marred torso with a
whimsical story, so
she could retreat to their room, so
they could catch her sympathetic tears with
fingertips, and become
who they needed to be.

**chronic fatigue**

bulb sessions unconscious, a
dribbling feed to the
inexhaustible pit at my
gravity-saturated center, a
creeping gas pedal to the
floorless gravitational slumber,
not with a splatter, but with a
fade

**green love letter**

i like the way you
hug at my diaphragm,
breathe through my body,
light through the needy, wound landscape and
leave it in the preferred dew of curious, by
monorailing red and white through
the clue board passageways
betwixt my neurons, the
secrets of which
one's own mind is
denied.

i like the way you
reduce me to my most
fundamental kernel,
etching lifelines back to the
me before the first fist, before the first finger, before
the first house-rehearsed lie was
confided in a soot eagle,
back to the snowy fuzz
pigtail, patchwork, library,
certainty that reality is
fallible.

i like the way you
swing the mossy cellar door from which
self-consciousness turns inner eyes,
only a neglected room large
enough for the big questions, for the
airing of antique dreams and nightmares, for the
sentient jungle curling through space,
and into the
modernized pastiche of
my best
self.

## nightmare II

the vilest nightmare is
not the one in which your shadow
crosses my porch rail, when i
throw two bolts and bury myself four wood rings deep
pounding a beckon to the sketchy, impassive national god
while outside the box, the cuddling air curdles as you
bleat for a second chance.

the vilest nightmare is
not the one in which your skeleton
slips among my congregation, when my
voice croons love's epitome and then ribbons tiny
with the light bulb of your intrusion blasting
chaos out of ceremony, gussied guests aghast as you
shriek for a second chance.

the vilest nightmare is
the one in which i come to in
a palm line purgatory, when i am in the stark middle of
a turgid hell's holiday of wholesale-humiliated catacombed children
bound to asphyxiation by your lavish, labyrinthine lies
because, thrashed and frigid, i
granted you a second chance.

## space between

the first time i put my hand inside you
my own teeth retreated beyond nervous throat
limbs dizzily shocked, the curtained illusion of distance
parted

infinitesimal circles commanded to halt
cupping feathers and chocolate, our ribs trembled in wait
paralyzed in honor of your stoic lion
heart

fates fade in the face of small sounds of breath
the lifelong campfire built by weathered fingers
the raw nerves that roar or sit, but remain
blazed

as your smooth aching gaze expands into a mirror
my outer shell scab blows into tiny stories
the ineffable space between two people finally
bridged

**the first**

*for the so-called silence breakers, finally heard*

later, i said he had half-fallen out of the cracked volvo door, leaning to howl at the cautious young basket of need paused on twin stilts upon the tooth-white strip mall concrete, flimsily shielded in last-gasp-of-the-horizon orange poly-cotton doodled with precise fuchsia studs in the outline of a magnified rose.

i am still waiting for the righteous empowerment particles lost in the air to coalesce into logic and action, to cause-effect punish the pupils and tongues who spread throughout misnamed public domains and fill their throats with unbreathable exhaust and inborn danger and the disillusion of a lighthouse-enforced lock.

i am still waiting for him to fall.

**to not get paid**

effective
as in, nodded at by a scrawny gatekeeper reverent to the single coin in his
    pocket
accepted into a fever dream of nobility shared by the fragile powerlines of
    martyrdom
the viscous acclaim of sparkle sans movement
a secret hissed through anonymous electronics
a minor deity bound to the goal of a paltry modicum of bowed scalps.

affirmed
as in, granted one dithering ghostly handshake
an extra scrap of blue polyester ribbon which does not survive the
    rideshare home
hours thrashed for the figurative privilege of nine additional tapped keys
    on a singular sheet of vanity pixels
no choice but to accept satisfaction in the loneliness of knowing
a feckless brag that evaporates into the charismatic storm clouds of my
    smaller yet brasher neighbor.

weightless
as in, i cannot keep myself on the ground to plot a traceable course
    around the board
cannot burn my ink into future records
floating as an inconsequential spirit through the tableau of my premature
    death scene
my hazy form shouting into the canyon without an echo
an impossible burden folding my single contributor's copy.

## hunger

*with thanks to Hiromi Goto, Clive Barker, and Ogden Nash*


the glueskin rictus maw swings ajar
to an inner beast isabel could not fool
ribs pangaea to a rickety carousel
intestines tap-dancing their way to a wring
fragile form inside out, clawing stopwatched need
prospect of pleasure gone flat for survival
roaring its ravenous pride as blocks drop from trees
and foal afterbirth dribbles down my parlor walls

**dentist**

i wait like a fictional baby-boomer
primed for detention with a
preemptive moral shadow for his
aw-shucks shenanigans.

i wait like an undercover journalist
sworn the other half of next month's rent to
impersonate a desk worker with a
self-described normal childhood.

you press at the tomes of my
last life as if mobs are not a minefield, as if
numbed by oxy-fluoride pellets to be a
housetrained practitioner.

you press at the reactive heartbeat of
each strand of marrow, and the
compacted decay of my twenties
volcanoes out like the inverse of an orgasm.

**winning**
>*with thanks to* So to Speak

performing my subtle reflex check at an unretailed moment, the contest message blinked shyly as any monotonous vibration.

i cannot source the pallet-printed conviction that grasped me when i saw the sender in pixilated calibri.

time through time, god and fate and non-specified spiritual plan left its beggars to sink through the marsh as i watched, right foot grounded, knitting ephemeral blankets of my skepticism.

and so, i cannot account for the click between my ears, before even the *congratula* preview, the muscle-eased knowledge: *this is it.*

the pessimistic or devout will hiss upon hapless reverence, a human urge to make ghosts of space dust and ignore oneself reverent.

i have another theory, and that is this:

despite the many-steepeled cage, secret strikes, and the blindfold between
  dawn and dusk,
the scarred breathing coils remain ever-hopeful.

and maybe this phenomenon is as vital as any faith.

**agoraphobic errand**

to deal with this fried ocean of
carbon-base, of dust and knives and
fingernails,

to deal with this yelling void, of
top-spinning gravity and a lyricless falling
up,

to deal with this mummy-wrap
laundry list of expectations and duck-rabbit
judgment,

with the logic of anxiety,
i will cloister myself in a tiny crunchable
box.

**sprung**

an innocent stroll
is washed over by daydream,
once-and-future sensation
amid fertile green.

the rolls of tape replay
our dewy rug burns
awaiting the hot lust gem
of summer.

cracked blossom releases
its fragrance to the breeze
in the heartbeat second
between look and beg.

sweating bullets and reservations,
i recall a belt of lightning
making colorful work of
my snowy mask.

and what a feeling!
curtains open,
the night pulls wet sounds out of us
and gulps them away.

## legacy

my mother once told me i was satan's daughter
a blight on a rubber ball crawling with god's six billion sons

i was, she insisted, each all-feared evil
stuffed into a misshapen, poisonous shell
which no number of sleep-starved ace grades would streamline
and no million hours of psalms could cleanse

i only asked half of the obvious question
*does that mean you're satan*, not *or did you fuck him?*
i only took the first layer of obvious conclusion
*you are broken*, not *my approval is a point-nine-barred fool's errand*

i reckon she deemed me a changeling, devil immaculate
as a mirror for the misery corroding her forehead's apple
as a freight train from holy strangers' appraisal of my watchmaker's nose
their sesame street humming and half-jokes about milkmen

rather than forgiveness, i aspire to righteous indifference
for my white-hot fear to soften into shrugged pity
to fly over each burning bush of wasted possibility
and the eternal martyrdom into which she is damned

**self-portrait dreaming**
*with thanks to Frida Kahlo*

unconscious,
i feel with every hair of my negligible
roots

papery
and forgotten in black and bleak pockets,
flammable

volumes
of history topple from their gravity-rooted
string

past
panoramas melded in geometric
anarchy

wedding
cake towers sprout from my decadent
splashing

unmapped,
the wakeful years since i paid an outlandish lung for
decorum

preexisting
stairways, the unlinked scandal of my
being

converted
to the webbed, throbbing veins of my
elephant

though
my compact carcass grows crowded, the gaps in my spiritual
limbs

still
i remain, absorbing soil from my bulbous inner
world

**witness**

sometimes, i wonder—not where you are, for my knowledge of your tiny world is sparse enough to make it a fool's errand—not who you are, because my flashbulb-pop memory can barely trace a linebreak from age to gender—but if you ever think of me.

eyes locked across the ocean from my airplane window, you looked—not confused, because your frozen irises understood the implications of his riotous raised palm—not unfeeling, because your knees emergency-broke in primal reflex—but helpless, misplaced.

when he let me fall out of his hands, you strolled on below the dizzy sun—not as if you hadn't seen, for you surely had—not with the hurried timber of finding help, for you surely weren't—alight in simplifying optimism.

a neatly dressed tourist grabs the smallest of three kids by the soft-forming ear, and i feel—not heroic, because the possum in my chest is assured of my own insufficient speed—not rageful, because the windstorm vibration of my blood shoves my voice box out of reach—but helpless, misplaced.

sometimes i wonder—if i have become you.

**dolores**
*with thanks to Duotrope*

*beautiful, beautiful, beautiful!* cry
the inflated patriarchs of academia, the
self-appointed poet boys pumping royal blood, the
cautious coeds at the outer crust of the
polished roundtable of mental masturbation.

to call me a victim, they counsel, is
to deny the infinite philosophical subjectivity of
the liminal space between my legs,
the single-socked sexiness of my entrapping youth,
my double-dutch skip from cradle to grave.

obvious depravity aside, they insist, acknowledged
for the sake of ignoring, for the class-honored trip of
magical writing and daring sensuality,
delve twenty pages deep into a brave mind that
can picture a predator, can rend its namesake a diminutive trope.

the amulet in an antihero's journey is
perpetually deemed dull: grail, vengeance, child.
surely, they say, i lost the right to protest the
narrative when i carelessly perished in initials,
undone by my first half-stab at legacy.

a century later, the nominal lesson grows
hazy
its sketched lines so perpetually undefined that
they rebuild me in the cultural imagination as
marilyn in miniature, an exotic
eastern taboo of preemptive autonomy

as if i could slip out of my caretaker-bruised skin and
gouged starving brain like a
careful tulle skirt, like a
provocative book cover, like a
fashionable adjective.

## now and then

seven years beyond my
scarred, starred young adulthood, you
were the slowest fellow floater in
my foreign dream city.
emotion-soaked calls from
across the expressway
demanded my presence,
raised an overture to which i
had not the heart chamber strength
to respond.

seven years beyond my
scarred, starred young adulthood, you
were the sparse reference point in
my philosophical freefall.
in an echoing studio of
bric-a-brac discontent, you
aired samples of a voice to which
i blanked my mind, a voice i'd have
swooned to in secret had it
belonged to a stranger.

now,
if i mention you at all
it's to gently laugh at your
theatrics, at the way my
budding queerness
shook at its cage
in our ill-fated kodak.

now,
i take stock of the way my
kid kernel jumps at
light on the river and
wonder what could have happened
if i had been
who i am now.

**the crash: a ptsd story**

on my second morning at the deli,
a second's shakes turned my meat carcass inside out. from
flood to combative meetings to
polka dot numbness, the
slipping sound echoed through the
caverns in my dreams.

during the first dance of my sixty-fifth show,
a throaty call froze my expected heels to the wood. with
plausible deniability held in public space,
muscles seized and surrendered,
revoked privilege of forgetting their
constant unsafety.

in the lit box oasis of chews amongst revelry,
a mob of donkeys swarmed to the other-marked victim. when
the fist inflated in my throat, the
nominal authority blinked at the beasts, passed my
nominal companion the vindictive spit of
fickle protection.

in the flashes i miss,
buttons sew themselves into my sleeves. i may
detonate at the secret word, the
café's closed corner kitchen, the
shine of a spectator's lenses, the
smell of bawdy grease.

crash.

**space**

i pictured an unending field of
starry, milky, vibrant
space, a set crackling with
energy and safely bound
limits, an instant feedback of
admiration, a self-aware heroism among
crucial technicolor discoveries.

i pictured the realm basking
deep in my mind, in which vibrancy does
not denote a slice of tragedy.

i dreamed of infinity finite to my
specifications, not still and chilled and
stagnant, not a regimented airplane of
governmental spins and extended
martyrdom, not a rock whose neck was
forever falling into the notched block for
the pompous sacrifice for grandchildren on
whom we vied to imprint.

i dreamed of fireflies resurrected, not
this arch, air-pricked demise witnessed only by the
viewfinder in my brain's moth-eaten leather.

**reclaiming**

what if i turned
your brand on my body,
the stark, puffy saw mark,
into beautiful, personalized art?

like a tattooed cancer survivor,
i could paint a world into your garish gap,
reclamation validated by
external visibility.

with the delight of a simple metaphor,
i could become portraiture education of
forbidden touches said not to count,
violation pardoned by law.

still, i know i will not.

to expand would be to accept
the sterilized hands that pried lesions into
my skin, the seven-layer scar tissue
hardened to rock via malnourished silence.

i prefer to unzip
your laceration, your ring of divide,
into sweatshirt and leggings, and
leave the messy puddle behind.

**i left because**

the intestinal pains of
my bank account are
lesser sharper purer than
the dead weight of silence, of
mythomanic mythology, of
self-shrinking martyrdom, of
stringing through an ever-constricting
vice of self-declared
holy.

i left because
i am no longer content to be
hungry.

**reptile rings**

the most popular fables in the world are anti-snake, illustrating the surly serpents as slaves to malicious chaos, if not evil personified. throughout fantastical semi-canon, wisecracking lizards, destined toads, and deadly masses of writhing id called dragons join forces, turn pages, demand loathing or respect. a sinister wisdom imbues the beasts' bellies like the heart of a lantern, commanding cultures to condemn sly wisdom as an unnatural threat.

our snakes, our dragons are flames and oceans.

the precious gems buried in my unblinking eyes, your fearsome claws shine selectively, on display to the other's flirty, beady gaze. composing a saga in furnace-toasted scales and blatant rebirth, their fear coalesced into a stale, chill air of loathing woven into the molecules of lungs. we slid from respective wreckages, cold blood as unlikely shield to the flooding flash fires, took stock of our new scars, and intertwined.

## hunger II

after wall-tallied seasons of mindful deprivation
and foam-eared ignorance after a model skeleton
the rockiest step is to anoint one's organs
a stark plastic hippo, a pulsing-rocked cavern

**dear jessica**

i use your real name only because
it's so popular, so purple on the speck of our
timeline, you joked, *a girl born in the
'80s? let's name her jessica!* and
scoffed at their commonness, you then
anonymous.

i let you hook to me, one
foot on the train, knowing i could
kindly, spindly, gently shake you but
dawdling throughout attachment,
suddenly desperate to be the obsession, the wolfe video
exception.

but meanwhile, my wayward foot never
came back, and your expectations faded into
an everworld silhouette,
phantoms in the air, hungers
not returned; instead, your string
burned.

we made the most of our
myth, the star-crossing lovers in different
'scapes, written, at long last, in our personal skies,
bodies busy like liberated intellectuals,
aching, twitching, throbbing,
bewitching.

through miles and my secret distance, we rehearsed
your practice-perfected moans reproducing their
grade behind my belly, your
educated checklist scrawled across
red sheets in my sweat, phone calls ending in
wet.

words tickled like tongues, so i
practiced the lines of my future, my fiction:

lick though your jeans, skin
humming like fingertips
in a voyeuristic crowd, being wanted a tangible
cloud.

i again tested my safe and
seductive hypothesis: i cannot be cracked by
one who cares more than i do—
this has, like most incantations, never shown to be
true.

i wanted it all: fireworks behind eyelids
emotions buffed and polished to an
earnest luster, while i hid my kernel deep under my
chest, bolt-secure in a place our
amorous explorations would not
excavate.

separated from our sighs and morning
dew, you admitted the elephant, my
cowardly remoteness. you
flitted my careless perch and
left me wary—we both deserved better. i'll always be
sorry.

**isolated incident**

when i learn of the second public shooting in a prior home sparsely known
for arid space and quiet crime, i wait.

national figureheads, who previously lambasted the brown bogeyman,
who harnessed the defenders of child trauma, default to stasis.
local ambassadors perform platitudes about lost innocence and community
unity, this unfortunate pitfall, this void behind a snowdrift of bullets.
the first gunman's foreignness is a cloud of bees, opaque and deadly, his
faith a gusting ghost out to rend congregations of paper dolls.
but the local boy, the gentle friend of sparse indulgence, with crosses and
baseball cards garlanding his dashboard?
well. he was married and overworked.

i wait by the omniscient window for someone with a louder timber to
notice, for a clouted cultural beast to comment, decry the discrepancy.

it comes, or it doesn't.

either way, i know we'll walk this lap again.
the time between draws taut and tiny with hopeless repetition, of troubled
individuals staring truth from magazines, of acceptable violence.
an immutable greek chorus spins its wheel between tragic genius and
    inevitable anomaly.
rustling two inches of newsprint, i listen to the wailers behind the wallpaper,
the guiding shapes proud between each typeset word.
after all, the spaces murmur, the everywoman, ever-expendable, should
    have seen it coming.
and to hear them tell it, she has disappointed us all.

**panic haiku**

rocks rise in my throat
insatiable lungs tremble
briefly, the world ends

**no soliciting**

we propel ourselves onto
graveled corners, cheap
pens pocketed in
hopes of the conscience of
strangers.

hours tick freeze blur with
the full-pocket hundreds
shaking heads, crinkling one dollar
bills at the odds of shooting stars or
lightning.

*you're doing good*
they say, and
we marionette smiles at the
vain alchemy of turning morale into
gold.

the sun is a hugging
madman, volatile as the
blue shade of
the crowd's politically pungent
sponge.

clocks scream our
sunset, our release into
two hundred steps to the
hybrid, a million times as
long.

*you did good*
i say, and
swoon with the heady rush of
activism, unless it's just the
bullfrog tang in my lower
eyelids.

**zoo**

thick spinning sweaters
doze, chatter hypnotically
instincts inspiring
my sludgy aorta

**orange day**

coded controversy was the sparkly spoon born into our shamed silent mouths.
hidden from sun and scars, we (almost) unite. this is gay pride, stand by me, or,
more to the point, the baby-sitters' club, the fuzzy femme speakeasy we dreamed
when first we tugged our cautionary sweaters over the rainbow patch on our
pants. lustful cheers, hugging mirrors, outraged objection, ointment
fly intervention are communal glue, a babel fish easing dangers,
intro for strangers.  until the journey to the cliff is waxed off
at the end, thirteen hours past your window, dregs a
shortened solo voyage back down the mountain,
like a compelling book you recited in
transnational unison but can
only reread
alone.

**dear mr.**

when i learned that you had officially deemed april sexual assault awareness month, shooting to smooth the selves silent with pre-friendly fire, to block the path of the faceless females so you might open a broken door and wait for gratitude, i preemptively shushed the white-hot coals melting into a mouth within my gut.

i became ice, because i know too much, wield too little, to examine the knotted void without eating myself alive.

i know how awareness sifts into a benign lump and is dismissed, bare-boned lip service to the impersonal others on the opposite side of the screen, congratulating yourselves with a voiceless motive which misses the wounded costars, and which reserves the lasting right to be revoked should a frostbitten martyr fail to beg.

i know how the domino erosion of trauma solidifies into a rock in a victim's bloodstream which may interfere in one's existence at the drop of a hand, the murkiness never to be eradicated from one's psyche, the conglomerates of criminally expensive oil waiting to erupt into a scribble on my self-worth.

i know the prolonged after-violence of witnesses and discoverers who lord the growth the spider hands planted as a lavish secret, like unpeelable dirty panties, like an unmovable dirty home, a trump card erected against my identity, spectator-crashed, each thin crust of comfort cracking into voyeurs vying for a broken doll fondled behind glass.

i know well that the bites from my body by the church man, the former friend, the strangers will never be as vilified as the wartorn lips of your teenagers, your employees, your ex-wives; how shrugging millions prop mine and condemn yours, misplace their charitable bandwidth for truth, because violence toward other bodies is a psychic grievance to be ignored, lilted noses up at the gumption i have to reject this inedible cherry on the freezer-burned backwash of your pittance.

because i'm aware. are you?

**fortune**

as a barely-concerned child, i
dreamed of a boy who believed
pleasure was like a pie graph. he
organized a mass kidnapping on the
fourth of july, so he might keep
all the joy of fireworks to
himself. i woke as evening fell, the
boy seated on an empty plain,
waiting to feel happy. at the time,
the tale struck whimsical, like an
aesop's fable. but in fact, a
dense rash mars my transcript of
passing faces, the times when
fortune adhered to my story. when
good news hit the air, i watched the
apparitions behind their eyes, took
stock of replies piled with panic and
razors, and thought
*oh. there he is again.*

**fireberries**

2012 marked the end of my world
a shattering of the snow globe into which my flesh was hatched

while redrawing skyscrapers, salting staid driveways
a pixilated blanket flowed with fruit

phoenix stencils, defiance, ephemeral safety
cropped into the hopeful freeze-frame of the future

a decade after i swore off the artistic needle
imperishable embers glowed back in my dreams

thighs blinking at sunset, i dared you to ask
you ducked from our textbook, evading shards

## adrenal fatigue

to wake up, i must
fight through ten meters of bats
as the runt caterpillar,
abandoned as un-fittest
on his brittle legs

air made of banshees, i am
an endurance slogan minus
the camera, absent the kids,
an uncongratulated martyr
with invisible rope

rocks laminate my
dissolving prey segments
and reform to subdermal pebbles
of deuterium, lesions eating
my single limping limb

## is it self-published?

tooth and throbbing shattered nail, i've
yanked my carcass by the baby toe joint over the
respectable cliff, to scale each trumpeted milestone and
manufacture an informed comment

and the strangest finding? the
landscape of strangers and colleagues who
melt into one wallpaper in their
desperation to believe it did not happen

the threat of the dwindling pie
the stubborn frame of alien professionalism
looms larger in their shadow selves than
stickers, than inches, than isbns

elbows pounding through atmosphere, i
pedal past tiny boxing rings
avoiding eyeballs with the inside-out ids
who would cast me their empty screen

**morning machine**

insistent gurgles drown out drips of progress
clouds of essence thrust up all neighboring spirits
winking sly promises to my caffeine-starved muscles

**robert did it**
*for the doll*

like so many personality-locket factoids, you presented your ancient self in the midpoint of my interactive window. desiccated face reveling in each blemish, permanent smirk content, proud.

well-known, but not enough. creepy, and too. a brand litmus test, a rube goldberg machine to keep unpalated tastes fenced at a distance. age-stopping supernatural shivers entice, tickle grins, beckon across highways, lime trees, and ozone gaps.

your form showed up larger, calmer than i expected. seuded skin offering resistance, a pinky-swear of either grace or havoc. endless onyxes reflected a mangy false lion, two-way mirrored the seductive mysteries of faith.

despite your stone gaze, my universe maintains a vast but finite fractal. i felled five hundred miles, four bridges, three audiobooks with my wayward tongue forming new roots in my cheek.

but when i shared your portrait, identical to any other but notable for the familiarity of my hands, the social dopamine machine awarded me nine *likes*.

drifting over the details, i see only eight names.

**intimacy is**

i was led to believe that
intimacy was a broken
thing, a thunderstorm mixing with the
grey waves as chests split into fire, the
penultimate moment a violent collision of baggage-strewn
pathos demanding averted eyes as
harsh cords swell to drown out
imperfect words and refit them with
comforting adage.
*i can't live without you.*

i was led to believe that
intimacy was not passing a surreal
hallucination back and forth like a
piece of chewed gum, speaking
truth oranges and
raggedy ann hammocks spinning through
safe space, as stubby
digits skate through the pooling cooling
sweat beneath my collarbone.
*my fingers are like little seals.*

they were all wrong.

**inside**

years passed of restrained placid pride
as i withheld the thrasher inside
then on one fated day
let spun rage out to play
and in separate corners, we cried

## flight

the maljams once soared free on earth and at home
curlicue flight patterns cool in the dusk
art and nests hidden in deep foliage
close and yet separate from land-dwellers' musk

spotted while bathing, an infant wrought panic
media, scientist, vigilante mass
too strange and firm for the old dreams of fairies
humans cried *threat* or *inferior class*

eyes iridescent, layered for each sense
long taste receptacle, elephant meets fly
though small and airborne, the strongest could never be
smashed by a fleshy hand, easy to ply

the humanoids hunted in militant pairs
riot gear marking their army of fear
team creature capture wrought poison and diligence
bent on streamlining the dark and the queer

*someday*, the parents coo to restless young
who stare, wistful, as the blue planet revolves
*someday we'll journey back and thrive in peace*
*soon as the dominant mammal evolves*

**holiday**

the nursery prism of credit cards rises yet taller
at ten a.m. when access fireflies blink red

the world of honest savings is tiny, monotonous
anonymous yet vital motor transmission

a knob-turning lamplighter stripped of french fable
i struggle to churn out last morsels of theater

to extract from the murky brew a suited parting
(the comforting adage, the one they expect)

i punch out and ascend, to clean with tonic and coffee beans
the hot spit of resentment from between my gums

## helliday

mid-college, my mind stumbled onto
a charmed article of scene décor:
it was cool to hate valentine's day.
my id could spin less conspicuously.

gaudy hearts beckoned with new possibility
with jolly long fingers in simple salute,
grocery store barbies gone sinister-fanged
to funnel cynicism into eccentric junk art.

the anti-capitalist rosebuds in our
brains raged over doxa's calculated tweaking,
brainstormed reclaims, v-monologues, madison manuals,
heckling gone holistic with authentic healing.

no one had to know there was another reason.

nine years young and abruptly very old,
i was alone with her in the house when
she pawed at the intimacies of the firstborn,
spirited off for habitual charity.

one note, one flamed gun with a
silver child-honed bullet: *if*
*they ever hit you again, call*
*me and i'll take you away.*

absent, her crimes were transposed onto me,
the life-size sickly dammit doll:
*how dare she? it doesn't count. i just do what i have to.*
the only noble lie was my golden silence.

it could have been any evening, but
i know that it wasn't, because after
she gave me a plush bear full of dry rose petals and
the last heart-shapes chocolates i would ever receive.

i said i wouldn't tell, and i
buried the toy beneath two-dozen
shoes in my closet, hoping
never to see it again.

**i miss those days**

before each phone alert felt like rocks in my tailbone
when twenty-one meant oysters, extras, and options
when jobs were feathered details for learning and lark

when homes lived by laws of journal visibility
when clutter read howard john hughes scene quirky
when livid tile footsteps bore no cross-country resemblance
to the sparkling layer in my upside-down basement

when i could muddle through an immaculate party house
each corkboard, each stool oozing pointed culture
without once mulling the stagnancy of
the jellied cash core creating each bannister

## thanks for nothing

i stare, amazed, at the decorated poet as he interrupts himself with anecdotes about his famous friends and wide travels. a peculiar irony hovers around my head as i struggle to picture employing the style tactics of this semi-star burning through the written word, and
ex-colleague audiences chuckling, rapt, the way they are in this room. i realize i can't.

i am not a forty-five-year-old straight man.

my voice is overconfident or timid, an overstepped velvet rope or a puppy's thirteenth yowl, not leading, strong, or assured, and never sexily cocky. but if i fail to smile at a grazed punch, if i weep or guffaw, will i sidle into an ungrateful other, a terrorist, man-hater, hurting the cause with a short-sighted blemish you set out to find?

i am not a forty-five-year-old straight man.

my sexuality is desperate and unsuccessful, because your eyes add the stage and i'm off-script from the shrugging notes left in your jacket pocket. but if my pen shares allusions to stinging hands, might i be brave or just whiny, a martyr, desperate for pity, the touchstone bitter for your exclusion, begging the blameless mob for an undue apology?

i am not a forty-five-year-old straight man.

i am childish, not young at heart
loud, not leading
snotty, not quiet
a namedropper, not well-connected
narcissistic, not sensitive
broken, not seasoned
insane, not quirky
brash for having produced a book before thirty and not a baby
and my voice is the special interest, as confidently assured by the faceless
pale default with the familiar desires and low voice.

so why even voice?

after all, i am not a forty-five-year-old straight man.

though i'm not meant to say it,
you may not be either.

**to the two twelve-year-old girls chuckling in the back of our honda**

on separate beaches, two troubled
oven timers declared us grown
decreed platitudes and clorox and the
swallowing of questions

city streets crisscrossed our noxious wrigglings
storybooks, gushers, and blatant pajamas
still we failed to sidestep the misshapen sweater of
responsible authority

when the new hit clicks on the car radio
you laugh as one note at
the self-affected dramatics
of commercial heartbreak

the punk empress has no skirt-suit
yet for the sake of structure
for stamina, for pyramids, for the
might of linear narrative

we swallow our snickers and
hide between palm lines
the truth that we are just
like you

Deb Jannerson's debut poetry collection, *Rabbit Rabbit* (Finishing Line Press, 2016), is a free-verse exploration of the power and fallibility of memory. Award-winning slam poet Franny Choi wrote that "[Jannerson] navigates sorrow, anxiety, and survival with the kind of lyricism that easily invites readers in," and *Autostraddle* praised it as "the perfect thing to read in the comfort of your room, any time you're longing to feel less alone." Her second book of poems, *Thanks for Nothing*, explores the biases of personal experience, the ways in which pop culture infuses one's personal narrative, and the far-reaching repercussions of political upheaval.

Jannerson won the 2017 *So to Speak* Nonfiction Award for her short memoir about queer intimacy and PTSD, and the 2018 Flexible Persona Editors' Prize for a piece of flash fiction about gruesome work injuries. She has also been awarded Honorable Mention for the Gival Press Oscar Wilde Award, received second place in the Pen2Paper Writing Competition, been a finalist for *New Millennium Writings'* Literary Awards, and been shortlisted for the William Faulkner—Wisdom Award.

More than one hundred of her pieces have been featured in anthologies and magazines, including articles for *Bitch* that were shared over 50,000 times. A graduate of the Cambridge Writers' Workshop, Deb is preparing for the release of her debut YA novel from NineStar Press. She lives in New Orleans with her wife and pets.

Learn more at www.debjannerson.com.

www.ingramcontent.com/pod-product-compliance
Lightning Source LLC
Chambersburg PA
CBHW021205090426
42740CB00008B/1235